POETIC VISIONS

HARVEY SPURR

Spurr Eden

Granville County

North Carolina

DEDICATION

Inspiration for creating poetry
often requires a muse.
Mine is my wife JB.

ACKNOWLEDGMENTS

HARVEY SPURR
is a fortunate fellow favored by family and friends.

Spurr Eden
Our ranch, where cattle and landscapes create poetic visions

OLLI at Duke
My association with the folks at
OLLI (Osher Lifelong Learning Institute)
at Duke University
contributed much to my development
as a poet.

Cover Design and Photos
by JB Spurr

AUTHOR'S NOTES

In a hurry?
This is not a quick read!
Read some
Contemplate some
Reread
Read aloud

Herein you will find sonnets, rhymes and
prose
Arranged as I can best fit
such an assortment

You choose as you like
and like what you choose

TABLE OF CONTENTS

TABLE OF CONTENTS
(continued)

SNUGGLING WITH SNUGGLEHEART

Songs, love poems to inspire, often so replete
'Compare thee to a summer's day', better my muse
Not the hot day, the best day, something complete
How to say, how to be, be not obtuse
Your kiss, tastes better than chocolate mousse
Your beauty, your charm, brought me to my knees
Your talent, my muse, inspires. I am Zeus!
'More temperate' by far, loving to please, to squeeze
Snuggling with Snuggleheart, O such felicities

NOTHING, DO NOTHING

Wake up, it's morning, you have a schedule
Look, your list, 'to dos,' nothing's left behind
You, you fool, you're caught up by your rule
Could be your mind, repose a bit, try, unwind

Think about your list, now your mind converges
Your required list, how much can you endure?
Look outside, envision where new life emerges
Outside sunshine and a pleasant temperature

You gaze out, mind drifting, forgetting work
Your schedule, your list, everything fades
Languishing, thinking, it seems so berserk
You see the place? The place where hope pervades

Nothing, do nothing, puzzle, struggle to clasp
Nothing, do nothing, now tighten your grasp

EDGE OF SLEEP

Sitting there relaxing in your chair
O so sleepy, your mind starts to wander
With eyes glazing you get fixed, you stare
Your thoughts drift, perhaps thoughts you'd ponder

On the edge of sleep now less than aware
You're conscious yet far away, asunder
Slow, flowing slowly, nothing to compare
As adventures pass by life seems fonder

A peaceful state of mind with all so clear
Moving toward a restful, enraptured spirit
Worries set aside, cast away all fear
Filled with quiet calm you cannot hear it

Your life can become peaceful when you choose
Come; give it a chance, what is there to lose?

THEN IS, NOW WAS

A place where green valleys and deserts abound
Here, then, goes way, way back to who knows when
Now look around and find our holy ground
In this far land, so close, now and again
People all grouped in many and various tribes
Mixing, complexity with constant strife
Difficult to address these contentious vibes
Duress cycles ripened each prophet's life
Among many, few, likely three who knew
Hearing sounds when heaven's voice came alive
One gave commandments, ten; another this clue
Beatitudes; last, five duties to survive
Moses, Jesus, Mohammed, here met their match
There's the catch, whom now, can God dispatch?

STUFF

What do you think…you do think?
Think of what
Money minded, honey minded, other minded
What do you think?
Not just conscious stuff
Subconscious
Drift away, move to space
Think about stuff
What you are, how you came to be
Ever stop to ponder?
You know, life
Whatever you define as life
You know, life and death stuff
Religious stuff
Stuff without answers
You might say mythological stuff
And, who does have answers?
But if you don't think about stuff
Does anything really matter?
You know, no thoughts, no stuff

WHEREART THOU O MY POEMS

I love poems and writing is hard, so far
"Twinkle, twinkle little star"
Looks easy, I do wonder what you are

Look at my words, my struggles, piles of rubble
"Double, Double toil and trouble"
Listen, descriptive rhythm and rhyme, I fumble

Try, yes, look at what I said, O, it hurts my head
"When I was sick and lay a-bed"
Writer's stress, I should stop and rest instead

Need to change, do something to ease the pain
"I must go down to the sea again"
Yes, now the words are coming, I see it plain

Now I have it, a wondrous verse, what can I say?
"Shall I compare thee to a summer's day?"
"O frabjous day! Calooh! Callay!"

COMPULSIVELY OBSESSIVE

What is my problem? I am a patient patient.
Whatever it is, nothing's for free, always a fee.
Worrisome, but then, I'm not complacent
Plainly stated, you say I have OCD.

I have an acronymic disorder? O me!
What? Obsessive-Compulsive Disorder.
This description, an encryption, surely.
 Such a long name, I wish it were shorter.

Certainly I'm fit, trim, my mind… my mind.
With the acronym, I might try to cope.
Common dysthymia occurs often you find?
The long name for shame discourages hope.

OCD is also known as disambiguation.
Horrible acronymic conflagration.

PABLO AND GERTRUDE

Easel and brushes, I put them aside
Paper and pen came with a tide

Poems, stories and prose
All these, must I compose

Create composition, master it all
Writing, writing, writing, dreading a fall

Grammar, grammar, grammar
Hits my head like a hammer

Want to, have to be free
Need to write as I see

Struggle, I struggle with all my might
Goals, achievement, are they in sight

My communion with word, my image, my chance
Now I ask, what is my stance

Oh Gertrude!?

Listen, listen to me, I must be a prude
Your stories, your prose, too, not too crude

Put down your pen, stay a cursive bent
Time to consider, encourage a prime talent

Take back your easel and brushes, start again the flow
And give us, yes, please give us, a PICASSO

TEEN TANGO OR A FANDANGO

Looking in the mirror what's to be seen
Staring back at me is clearly a teen
Continue this stare, a smile makes it pleasant
Lightens my face, my lips in a crescent

Have a group date, time is short, can't wait
Fast changes without debate or I will be late
Eyes shadowed in azure blue, they should be green
To look better, match my hair with heightened sheen

This hair is like the others, though mine has a little furl
A bit of curl, well, kind of a swirl
My face, prepared all in haste, is not up to my taste
O to shower and bloom again like a flower, no time to waste

Jeans or skirt, I wonder, should I flirt
Careful is best, stay in arrest, contain being hurt
My date, an attraction, could lead to some action
In zippered jeans a retraction, could diffuse my reaction

There's much to consider, no time to dither
Have to go hither, wish I could twitter
I'm ready now, where are my friends, O so slow
Doing the things I know, I go with the flow, I am the show

And God help me tonight, keep me in sight
As I use all my might, to do what is right
Looking back in the mirror, when this is done
I'll remember this fun and be glad I'm twenty-one

ODE TO A SMALL STONE

I reached down, picked it up by hand
It's a stone, just a tiny, little, small stone
There in the road, itself not alone
With a million, a zillion there on the land
Here on the road, from where did it come
Perhaps a far off quarry, hauled by truck
Crushed from a parent rock, such is the luck
A small stone similar to, yet different from some
Rocks and stones are taken for granted
Mostly unseen as we tread down the road
Lying with others, flat, bearing our load
Just one stone among many vital to this planet
    Now in my hand in the sun it glistens
    Glad to be admired quietly it listens

HISTORY OF MANKIND

Irate
Full of hate
Take aim, spit
Make a hit
Grab a rock, throw
Strike a blow
Load a gun, fire
Destroy desire
Launch a rocket
Smash the threat

Irate
Annihilate
Exterminate
Perfect your aim
Confront your fame
Mankind's shame

AS EVENING SHADOWS LENGTHEN

Day moves on as evening shadows lengthen
Locked in romance, our love does strengthen
Moving close, touching, our hearts do embrace
Loving in comfort, surrounded by God's grace
We do envision our world as verdant, green
A bright blue sky, so clear no clouds are seen
With incense and flowers, such sweet perfume
This world for you and me, we must consume
Hard to describe love without a tether
This force to bring us, hold us together
Joined in shining love we are ignited
Everywhere we touch we are united
   Your presence an overwhelming essence where
   You, so lovely, so fair, you, without compare

TWITTER & TWEET

Birds of a feather flock together
Wherever and whatever enjoying fine weather
Many feathered friends may join in the beat
Singing, tweeting with pleasure, sounds abound
Tethered together all belong, sharing in song
Twittering and dithering the music is sweet
All the little birdies go tweet tweet tweet

Now, other birds unfeathered, ungathered, scattered
Make no chirps or sound, also abound
Not just in pasture or wood, all over, wherever
Eyes down, glued, fingers flitter
Posting silent tweets on Twitter
Selective sensitivity, characters, no more than one-forty
Communication complete, message replete
Subtle tweets, tweaked, twittered feat

Birds to ur phone U C B4 U a tweet
All the little birdies go tweet tweet tweet

SPURR EDEN MUSE

Eyes closed, I imagine
Spurr Eden
Granville County therein

Pastures, woods, engulf space
Peaceful place
Nature carefree in grace

By an oak stands my Muse
Tis God's whose
Tree and beauty diffuse

Cows watching, their eyes bright
All in sight
Calm, silent, without fright

Quietly she whispers
Sweet vespers
Listen, her trust transfers

With this Muse at my side
I confide
Poems arise where we reside

THANKS GIVING

Every year when late November draws near
There's this Thursday, to many Oh so dear

Goes back in time to English Puritans
National holiday, Thanksgiving fans

Of late, families held a turkey feast
Eating and providing for those with least

Recent intrusions have crimped turkey time
Starting somewhat small, the focus sublime

Friday, then Thursday, now, camp out Wednesday
You know what I mean; it is 'Black Friday'

So our thankful day gradually loses sway
Giving way to fond hopes of stretching pay

Hurry. Get gifts for this December bash
It's someone's birthday. Still holding some cash?

You didn't miss the bargains, go online
There's 'Cyber Monday' for what you pine

SPRING? NONSENSE

Ouch! That hurts, you pinched hard, it will swell
Time to get up, you're late, where's your bell?

You're crazy, it's not time, and you're terrible, untoward
Aha! Didn't change your clock, you know, "Spring Forward"

Spring forward my foot, listen, that wind is blowing
Wow! Look, horizontal snow, the "March Lion" is showing

Spring? Crazy, I wonder, where are the birds and bees?
Who knows, hiding out I guess, avoiding a certain freeze

Listen, the neighbor's rooster is crowing, doesn't know the time
All clouds, no sun, he's having fun, listen to me, I rhyme

I'm hurrying to dress, best I can, Whew! What's the smell?
Well, bread stuck in the toaster again, it's burned to a shell

Yuk! What to eat, I suppose it will be the same old cereal
That or nothing, it's your fate, hurry up, you're unreal

Spring, oh spring, please come hence
It's about to break, I can tell, my sixth sense

MISSING,
THIS WORD DESCRIBING THIS THING

On the tip of my tongue, a word, on which I'm hung
It describes for you this object, a thing, quite far flung
I know this word, one you know, you've heard
Funny, it left my mind, flew away like a bird

If the bell in my head would ring
I'd have the word that describes this thing
Wordless, I think, how best to describe this object
Looking at it now, wow! Believe me it's a project

It has neither structure nor form
What can I say; with certainty it's not the norm
Not standing nor lying, not sitting nor reclining
Not bright nor shining, can't say it's dull or hiding

You wonder at the shape on which I gaze
It's sort of, very unusual, a bit of a maze
It makes not a sound but it's hanging around
It's both in the air and on the ground

It has no color, no texture, no smell
At least none from what I can tell
Not intending to be offending or sound quite confused
You may wonder what it is, but are not too enthused

Could be more, could be less, more could be less
Puzzling I'm sure, this thing that fills my consciousness
O! Now I remember, of course, let's stop all this fuss
The word I'll shout until I am hoarse, is amorphous

17

FINDING LOVE

A young Harry liked to play outside
His Mom had to call him once or twice
And maybe again, slow response, I confide
Although a good boy, one call should suffice

Finishing high school, Harry needed work
When Mom called once her sink drain was stuck
Harry grabbed a plunger he didn't shirk
Once, twice this expunger cleared the muck

Harriett called Harry in her duress
Her commode had exploded she did scream
Harry came with plunger, once, twice, success
Hugs and kisses were more than he'd dreamed

Now in business, he's a plumber
Harriett's his wife Harry's no dumber

FLAG THE TRAIN

Tall and thin, a lad, no one we knew had
Ever stopped a train, not in pouring rain
The idea was bad, even the thought sad
Standing there so plain, just gave me a pain

Trains go fast, few stop, can't recall the last
Small station, not lit, no facilities, just unfit
Had to raise the mast, quick, before it passsed
Not easy, not a bit, stand, no where to sit

Help, no station crew, not safe where trains flew
Wonder from where he came, stop a train here - lame
The wind really blew, short time, the train due
Mast up all the same this lad with no name

Then the whistle blew we heard and we knew
Wheels screeched, this night it stopped all right

WONDER, EVER WONDER

Wonder, wonder from where you really came
Wonder, as you search the world for knowledge
Truly you're smart, knowing is your hedge
So, you know your name, so what's your fame
Current knowledge defines your existence
Ever wonder what ancient people knew
Old prophecies often provide a clue
To conscious presence, a woeful subsistence
Perhaps you're blessed and see the light
The light so bright it conceals the Spirit
This light's on you, quiet, now you see it
Shining on you, helping, finding your sight
   Now shine your light to create new fame
    Wonder, now, from where you really came

DEFINING YOUR GOD

Defining your God, is such your plight
Confusing, perhaps it's out of sight
For some a concept containing delight
Still others may think it is not our right
Difficult to express, are you contrite?
Answering requires most of your might
To heck you say, I'd rather fly a kite
Whatever your stance, not ever a slight
As every day ends, you face the night
You could be thinking, try to see the light
Comprehend and feel, reach for a new height
Follow this path with increased appetite

Opened mind, loosened strings can't be tight
Stay, steeped in comfort, no need for flight

STEP ON A DUCK

Onomatopoeia! Momma mia!
Crazy, silly syllabification
This tongue teasing, pleasing phenomena
This syllabolic discombobulation

Noise words are around, try a sample sound
Be still, listen. We open Champagne: POP! FIZZzzz
Whoo, whee! you exclaim when a treasure found
You see, you're a whizz, now a little quizz

Try this: you step on a duck--quoo wack
Good sound! Onomatopoeia do abound
Pinch someone--Saalapp!, Sit on a tack--
Ooouch! You're on track, a talent profound

Master the subtle, je ne sais quoi
Momma mia! Onomatopoeia!

HOW'S YOUR MORNING COFFEE?

Mine is good
Made my way
Right coffee
Right water
Tastes right

That's not all
Our setting
We sit well
Together
Morning prayer
Kiss and hug

Now then
Right time
Sip and pause
Pause and sip
Life's elixir

How's your morning coffee?
Mine is good

FIRST AND LAST

First, you want early on, what does it mean?
Front of the line, first at the fountain
Climbing hard, first to top the mountain
Winning the race, being first, does seem keen
You know the number, it is…O…N…E
Another one is double…U…O…N
Stacked up firsts, displayed in your den
All in order, one and won, a quantity
Groomed early, you developed this thirst
Rushing, working, pushing, you had to be first
Older and slower, you could slip to last
Now what is your chance, how is the die cast?
  So the last shall be first, and the first last:
  For many are called, the chosen march past

POETRY WORKSHOP THURSDAY,
WRITE A POEM

Poetry workshop Thursday, write a poem
Perhaps a swell villanelle, make a name
Polish, polish, polish, shine it like chrome

Once finished and presented, I'll go home
Could fail, such would spoil my fame
Poetry workshop Thursday, write a poem

I could quit now, maybe travel to Rome
Do it fast, get it done, don't be lame
Polish, polish, polish, shine it like chrome

Can't get the beat, need a metronome
Lacking rhythm and rhyme, am I to blame
Poetry Workshop Thursday, write a poem

Need help, where's my friend the gnome
Might seem easy, O yes, you try this game
Polish, polish, polish, shine it like chrome

Here, finished, it is from my dome
Print it out and put it in a frame
Poetry workshop Thursday, write a poem
Polish, polish, polish, shine it like chrome

LOVERS RECOVER, THERE'S PEANUT BUTTER

Ever get caught cause you're a lover
Had to run and look for cover
Found your nerves all in a flutter
And you didn't know about peanut butter

There, held tight in her embrace
Your hands all tangled in lace
Found by another, stronger lover
You'll need some peanut butter

Seen a ghost, you shake more than most
Don't be a flake or crumble like toast
There's hope like words from Mother
It's there in a jar of peanut butter

For children there's smooth and creamy
For the hearty there's crunchy and munchy
In this matter you'll need the latter
It's my druthers use real peanut butter

Getting caught is nothing new
Happens to many, not just a few
All these others, they did recover
But only after eating peanut butter

Now's not the time to shirk
We know it's going to work
Quick, off with the cover
Time to eat some peanut butter

There, you're getting better I know
Your blood is starting to flow
Looks like you'll recover
Thank God for peanut butter

With another sweet face
You're back in the chase
Held tight in her embrace
Your hands all tangled in lace

Please don't get caught again my lover
Especially without your peanut butter

DO EXPLICITLY

Don't do as I do
Do as I say

How do I do
If you do another way

You know what I do
But that's not what I say

I see what you do
Yet find another way

Do do to what I do
Do do what you want to do

Phooey, let's try again to do
Don't get carried away

I know, don't do what you do
Do a different way

Yes, that's what you do
Something other I say

Pooh! I'm tired of what you do
Too exhausted for another way

BEFORE...AFTER...NOW

Before, before, before, what came before?
You. You're older; tell me, what did you see
Your mind, your experience, your folklore
Was there order? Disorder? Share it with me
After, after, after, what comes after?
Who has been after? Tell me what they say
Prophetic claims of afterlife or disaster
If you know, tell me, do it without delay
Now, now, now, the present, it's here now
I see, I hear, I touch, all these I sense
Reason and talk, all my time will allow
I see many who trust in Providence
Before and after, believing, not seeing
Now, spirit and existence are my being

WHERE I COME FROM, WHAT'S IN A NAME

Yes, I can tell you from where I came
And, make it sound good, that's my beat
First though, who gave me my name?

When Dad was born, Grandpa lived on a street
His brother, Dad's uncle, on another
Combined street names for Dad, a real treat

Next, my turn, Dad consulted Mother
Decided on junior, more's the pity
Then came three sisters and a brother

In a small town, near a big city
All knew your business, seemed the rule
But, be there to help, singing a ditty

We kids shared colds and the flu, often cruel
Learned to play, seeking and hiding in nooks
You stay on the path otherwise you're a fool

Mom and Grandma, boy, they could cook
Knew the time, wondrous odors filled the air
Prepared from memory, don't remember a book

Dinner at the table, all children were there
With clean hands and face, don't be late
Thanks for our plenty, time for talk, to share

Finish your food, want to go, carry the plate
Plenty of chores, do your part, nothing neglected
Pulled sisters' hair, got scratches, that's your fate

Attend school, do lessons, that was expected
Parents and grandparents set the example
Be courteous to grownups, teachers were respected

Church on every Sunday, Dad was a deacon
He saw us there, dressed in our best, all five
We saw the light; it was bright, a clear beacon

Now we're much, much older, still much alive
We miss Dad, Mom's reached ninety-five
We've moved on, but our town does survive

But what of my name and from where I came
Name doesn't matter, it's to family we owe our family

ADRIFT

Horse in the pasture
Boat at the dock
Book on the shelf

grass   water   silence
alone   parked   stacked

Nobody rides the horse
Nobody sails the boat
Nobody reads the book

Clasping nothing   grasping nothing
In the clouds
Adrift

I AM COUNTRY

I like the country, filled with animals
Longing for my sounds, the croaking of frogs
Here in this city, likely cannibals
Can't think now for the barking of dogs
Many tall buildings surrounded by shops
Night in this city is flooded with lights
Everywhere you are watched, lots of cops
So needed to stop the scuffles and fights
Suddenly covered by hard rain showers
Gave up walking, moved on in a taxi
Through water-filled streets void of flowers
Slow-moving traffic, life's not fancy
   I miss the country, the winding creeks
   Flowing through the ever green mountain peaks

ELLA WATER

Ella has water
Lots of water
Water in the sink
Water in the tub
Water in the washer
Water in what you think
Water water water, water everywhere

Ella pulls plugs
Ella turns knobs
Water swirls down
Water disappears
Goodbye water, so dear
Water's gone, all is cheer
Water water water, water nowhere

Whoa! What you didn't expect
What disappeared has reappeared
Back in the tub, back on the floor
A sudden impact, a tremendous effect
Ella is hurrying, Ella is scurrying
Grab a sponge, grab a mop
A fecal mess, a total sop
Water water water, water everywhere

O me, O my, wish I could fly
It's all on me, I have to try
Can't sit on the seat I have this fear
A back flush contaminate will hit my rear
Call sister for advice, "Get a bigger septic tank!"
Sure, sure, that's nice, do I look like a bank?

Met this nice plumber, maybe we can deal
Came in a flash, a smile so brash, what appeal
"I'll get to the root of your problem"
Looked and hooked a big root from a sweet gum

Water water water, water nowhere
Water's gone, all is cheer
Water logged with my plumber dear

YEARNING TO SONNET

Exercise: write fourteen lines, a sonnet
You can do it now, complete, without fear
Write nothing stupid like "scratch your bonnet"
A week will do, make it up, bring it here
Petrarch's method or Shakespeare's invention
Similar in rhyme, differing lyric form
Singing with rhythm, familiar convention
Take a stab, write anew, make it the norm
Need A B A B then C D C D
All in i am bic pen tam e ter
Then E F E F finally G G
Crazy it seems, containing my laughter
  So early in life there is baptism
  So later in life why not sonnetism?

INDIFFERENT

Indifferent?

No interest
No concern
No feeling
No emotion

No matter

Immovable
Immobile
Immutable
Impassive

Apathetic
Not involved
Not required
Not obligated

Not this
Nor that
Neither
Neutral

Could
Should
Would

Perhaps
Maybe
Possibly

Indifferent

PRESERVE A JAR

I washed it
I washed it in the dishpan
I washed it after
I washed the other dishes

I don't know why I washed it
It seemed there must be some value
Some value I could not immediately grasp
I felt it was there

I stood at the sink
Hands immersed, grasping the jar
Rubbing to clean it, wondering what I had
Wondering, why was I doing this?

I was scrubbing it
Cleaning away the clinging surface
The innards went fast, a few scrubs and rubs
The inside was clean

It was the outer-pasted paper
I scrubbed and rubbed
Surely the hot water, the soapy, hot water will penetrate
Surely these pasted paper labels, will float away

They did not
They clung to the surface
They clung for dear life
I rubbed, I scrubbed, I scratched

Little by very little
Little scrape by little scratch
They succumbed
They curled in the wash water

Losing their identity
Losing their name
Losing the instruction
Losing their source

Finally, I stopped
I had not succeeded
There were traces of adhesive still
On this clear glass jar

Traces of its past
Traces of its origin
I dried it, replaced the lid
Why, I was not sure

I placed it next to a green, clean wine bottle
On the counter top
Where…the early sun
Penetrates them both

I sit here and stare and wonder
Why did I scrub a jar?
What was the reason?
What makes sense?

It had a purpose
It held preserves, strawberry preserves
They were sweet
They embellished my taste

I remember their selection
Jelly, jam, preserves, all there on the shelf
Did I know the distinctions? I was not sure
I went with preserves, not that I don't like jelly

And now
I stare at the glistening jar
Lid in place, dispensing sunlight
I stare, I wonder why

WHAT'S IT…THAT'S IT

It. Just two letters i and t
Stop to think just for a bit
Without it, where'd we be?
It here, it there, it all to wit

Learned it early, it's English first
Third person singular, it's neuter gender
Remember gender? It's the worst
It, the thing, a nonhuman contender

It he, it she, it the proper pronoun
It is she, he did it, and, it was polite
Correct it is, you get it, hands-down
You know: it was over, does it right

Its possessive and it's a contraction
It's raining, he'd had it, a thing it tis
It's tiring compiling its didaction
You know it, aw, gee whiz

If you'd start it with capital I
This it could be the big It, sigh

LESS MUCH LESS

Restless
Senseless
Restlessness

Motionless
Mindless
Quest less

Listless
Never the less
More or less

Restless
Senseless
Restlessness

WORDS, JUST WORDS

You have noticed, certain words have their say
Describe objects, things: a bird sings then wings
You get the picture, bird songs, sights and flings
And now, indeed, what else do words convey?

They make smiles and laughter come alive
Provide messages from past generations
Crystallize our thoughts, views and sensations
Words, just words, used wisely help us survive

Curse dull prose, so depressing, nothing worse
Words this way bad, that way sad, mundane
The common, usual phrases we disdain
Better short, terse, perhaps a rhyming verse

As morning dew mistifies, what do we eschew
Continue on, for there is no curfew

A PATH

I am on this path, this path that I tread
Unsure where it leads, a feeling of dread
A way for me needs to be traveled
A way to reveal my soul unraveled
Moving forward, this path a slippery slope
Filled with obstacles, I try to cope
A scary challenge, this is my plight
Searching, looking ahead there is a light
From the void, a sudden steady voice
Give me your hand you have a choice
Moving hand in hand the light grows brighter
My spirit rises, the grip grows tighter
Now a light within gives rise to vision
My soul restored, seeing with precision

BO PEEP SHEEP BLEEP

Little Bo Peep has lost her sheep,
And doesn't know where to find them;
Leave them alone, And they'll come home,
Wagging their tails behind them.

Old Chief this dog day was tired of new tricks
Resting, he enjoyed peaceful Mammalville
Where, as a police dog, he took his licks
And now heads the K-9 force with dogged skill.

BARK! BARK! HARK! HARK! Came a couriers cry
"Doggone dog day!" Chief growled a long doggerel.
"What's the fuss, message Guy?" Chief did sigh.
'Gone! Bo Peep and sheep! I have come to tell.'

"Go and fetch 'Dog the Dick.' He'll get the scent."
"Dick! Go see Bo's Mom, get the smell and trail."
'OK Chief, they're lost again is no accident.
Another Bo Peep Sheep Bleep seems a fairy tail.'

Bo's Mom, Mo Peep, works cheap as a housekeep
Dick asked: 'Where's Bo? Think she's gone far?'
'She leaves the sheep, takes the jeep to see this creep
And wags her tail as he plays guitar at Sonnet Bar.

45

When Bo's gone I think Black Sheep leads the keep
Follows the deep seep down by the Overleap.
I need Bo to come home to upkeep so I can sleep
Bills are steep. Pa Peep's hurt, can't chimney sweep.'

Sonnet Bar barkeep pointed Dick to Bo Peep
Gone were guitar and jeep, she was fast asleep
Dick nudged her gently. Awake, she did weep.
"I'm sorry for all. As I sowed, I did reap!"

Stanza 8

Forlorn! The very word is like a bell
To toll me back from thee to my sole self!
Adieu! The fancy cannot cheat so well
As she is fam'd to do, deceiving elf.
Adieu! Adieu! Thy plaintive anthem fades
Past the near meadows, over the still stream,
Up the hill-side; and now 'tis buried deep
In the next valley-glades:
Was it a vision, or a waking dream?
Fled is that music---Do I wake or sleep?

Stanza 9

With sleepy vision I awake to travel hence
My emboldened soul has fenced with death
Time for me to seek and find recompense
I am bestowed before my final breath
O bird of wonder, your song is in my heart
With uplifting rhythm its treasure inspires
Though nightly you wander carried by Poesy
Awakened to respond, I must start
Writing verse and rhyme as to my desires
So all may share my words with empathy

Stanza 8 Ode to a Nightingale by John Keats
Stanza 9 reply to *Stanza 8* by Harvey Spurr

TIME AND AGAIN

What is the time, I ask, you are unsure
You look for a device, need to be precise
What is time? It holds a strong allure
Feigning when and then, slippery as ice

Time seems so common, common to this life
Hearing all the time, your time, my time
Part time, half time, makes all a time of strife
No time, a lifetime, yes, time must be prime

You remember when, plan for then perhaps
Estimate your time, what is your measure
Try. Get it in your grasp, avoiding a lapse
Wasting time causes you much displeasure

So, time moves on, can't stop, no, never
Then, endless time, God's time, is forever

SPRINGING SPRING

Clear cold
Crystals sparkle
Clustered on
Concrete walks

White snow
Slush
Gray mush
Muck

Wintry winds
Wither
Grasping gasping
Winter whimpers

Wishing for warmth
Sensuous signs
Sunshine
Springing forth

Early Easter
Flurries chills
Easter later
Daffodils

Refreshing rains
Rhapsodic
Dramatic
Ecstatic

Slowly soaking
Soothing season
Simmering soon
Summer solstice

49

WINTER WEARY

Soft white flakes, descending, seeming to float
Land gently, gradually covering all
Transforming, changing landscapes, hiding fall
Bringing pleasure, soothing, sensual coat
Sitting by the window my eyes a glaze
Mind drifting, light as air, holding a stare
Wonderful feeling, wishing, like to share
Not moving, wanting to stay, in a daze
Reality, first snow, second snow, not last
Slippery walks, iced streets shrouded by salt
Another snow, goes for days, please do halt
Tranquility moves to tranquilized, fast

My white beauty, all transformed, now dreary
Snowing again, I am winter weary

MY LOVE FOR YOU

I come not in brief or a fling
Nor with sweet verse to sing
No braided gold as a ring
It's mighty, a stronger thing
I hold, have and will bring
This passion to forever cling

52

ABOUT THE AUTHOR

Harvey Spurr is a poet, rancher, scientist
who lives and creates in
Granville County, North Carolina,
much to the delight of JB,
his wife and muse

PREVIOUSLY PUBLISHED

Pablo and Gertrude; Preserve a Jar; Yearning to Sonnet
Published in *Thursday's Poems*, OLLI Poets Workshop 2010,
Osher Lifelong Learning Institute,
Duke University Continuing Studies

*Compulsively Obsessive; Lovers Recover, There's Peanut Butter;
What's It...That's It*
Published in *Life Lines,* OLLI Poets Workshop 2012
Osher Lifelong Learning Institute,
Duke University Continuing Studies

www.ingramcontent.com/pod-product-compliance
Lightning Source LLC
Chambersburg PA
CBHW060429050426
42449CB00009B/2207